Dan Poynter has done it again! *Para Promotion Program* is an idea factory for any author. Each chapter is loaded with easy-to-apply information. Get this book and then take 15 minutes a day and actively apply one suggestion to your own book. Watch your results explode.

—W. Terry Whalin, best-selling author
of over 60 books including *Jumpstart Your Publishing Dreams, Insider Secrets to Skyrocket Your Success*

There are a plethora of reasons why Dan Poynter is the go-to thought leader on successfully and PROFITABLY writing and publishing your book. His new book continues that tradition with a "paint by the numbers" approach on that strange and exotic world authors have to enter after an immense effort to birth their passion in a newborn book. Ignore him only if you want to write off the financial, emotional, and personal investment you made in your unique book.

—Gary W. Patterson, the FiscalDoctor®
www.Fiscaldoctor.com *Million Dollar Blind Spots: 20/20 Vision for Financial Growth*

Anyone who has written/published a book in recent years knows that the promotional landscape is constantly changing as new techniques and technologies are being developed; consequently, becoming aware of, not to mention trying to learn, these new promotional techniques can be a very daunting task. Luckily though, Dan Poynter, one of the world's leading experts on self-publishing—or "Indie" publishing as many refer to it these days—has decided to share 51 ideas to help you navigate your journey. Many of the ideas are free (or inexpensive) and they are easy to implement; therefore, you not only save time and money, you also start to actually enjoy doing the activities! No, that's not a typo. I found it to be quite interesting and fun to complete the different activities.

Let's be honest, we tend to avoid doing things that we don't understand and we avoid undertaking activities that are painful or frustrating and for many of us promoting a book falls into one of those categories. The *Para Promotion Program* is the first book of its type in this new digital era (that I am aware of) and it truly is a step-by-step guide that anyone can use and everyone can benefit from. And, due to the fact that many of the activities can be learned before your book is completed, you can hit the ground running when your books are ready to go out into the world.

—**Karl Schmidt, author,**
photographer, student of life

I was in Guatemala, so far from "home" and what I thought was the logical book market, that I came across Dan's 51-week lesson plan for turning my book into a money making enterprise, instead of an idea whose time (apparently) hadn't come yet!

With the Dan Poynter plan my book came back to life in no time. I realized that with learning Dan's secrets I could make a name for my book and myself and make a very healthy contribution to my income.

What is most amazing to me is that neither age nor location made the least bit of difference in following Dan's step-by-step process to promoting my book. I'm far from young and living in a third world country. Yet every word of Dan's lessons is completely understandable, do-able and relevant for ME. His wonderful guidance is one of those magical gifts that totally works—if you work it!!

—**Linda DeBlanco, author of**
Get Packing: If Not Now, When?

About this Book

Writing a book is a creative act but promoting a book is a business. The *Para Promotion Program* gently introduces authors to the business side of books.

Dan Poynter's *Para Promotion Program* is a series of book promotional projects the agoraphobic author can accomplish without leaving home and shows the author what to do to reach their audience. Each assignment takes five to 120 minutes to complete. The program not only shows the author how to promote his or her current book, it is a crash course in book promotion that can be applied to future books. And authors who understand how to reach their audience tend to write books their readers want.

The Para Promotion Program is far more valuable and much less expensive than traveling to a conference or seminar.

The Para Promotion Program is the brainchild of Book-Publishing Futurist Dan Poynter of Santa Barbara. Poynter says: "The challenge is that most of us authors are introverts. We prefer not to take part in radio, TV, or autograph parties. So, I assembled a team of PR and book design professionals to design a procedure acceptable to (homebody) book authors."

About the Author

Dan Poynter is the author of more than 130 books, has been a publisher since 1969 and is a Certified Speaking Professional (CSP).

His seminars have been featured on CNN, his books have been pictured in *The Wall Street Journal,* and his story has been told in *The New York Times.*

The media come to Dan because he is the leading authority on book publishing. Often referred to as The Book Futurist (and ebooks are the future), he is the most-often quoted authority on book publishing today. Dan is the sponsor of the Annual Global eBook awards

Dan travels more than 6,000 miles each week to share, inspire, and empower writers, publishers, and professional speakers through keynotes and seminars. Thousands of best-selling authors have profited from Dan's advice.

"One essential ingredient to our Chicken Soup success was consulting with Dan Poynter in the early stages."
—Jack Canfield, co-author
Chicken Soup for the Soul series

Dan Poynter's
PARA PROMOTION PROGRAM

Dan Poynter's
PARA PROMOTION
PROGRAM

A Step-By-Step Guide
To Successful Book Promotion
For Authors & Publishers

Foreword by Ellen Reid

Para Publishing
Santa Barbara, CA

 Para Publishing
PO Box 8206
Santa Barbara, CA 93118-8206
Tel. (805) 968-7277
http://ParaPublishing.com
http://ParaPromotion.com

Printed in the United States of America

Publisher's Cataloguing-in-Publication Data

Poynter, Dan.

Dan Poynter's Para promotion program : a step-by-step guide to successful book promotion for authors & publishers / Dan Poynter ; foreword by Ellen Reid. -- Santa Barbara, CA : Para Publilshing, c2015.

    pages ; cm.

    ISBN: 978-1-56860-165-6 (paperback) ; 978-1-56860-166-3 (eBook)
    Summary: Writing a book is a solitary act. Selling a book requires the outgoing gregariousness of extroverts and therein lays the conflict. This book is designed to educate authors and bring attention to their books. The system starts with scores of tested ways to promote books. It will work for print books, ebooks and books available in other editions. Authors will discover how to promote their current book and their next and their next.
    --Publisher.

    1. Books--Marketing--Handbooks, manuals, etc. 2. Authorship-- Marketing--Handbooks, manuals, etc. 3. Self-publishing--Handbooks, manuals, etc. 4. Electronic publishing--Handbooks, manuals, etc. 5. Publishers and publishing--Handbooks, manuals, etc. 6. Authors and publishers--Handbooks, manuals, etc. I. Reid, Ellen. II. Title. III. Title: Successful book promotion for authors & publishers.

Z283 .P69 2014   2014954281
070.5/029--dc23   1411

Book Shepherd and Book Producer: Ellen Reid, indiebookexpert.com
Cover & Interior Design: Ghislain Viau, CreativePublishingDesign.com
Cover Photo: Kim Gottlieb-Walker, Lenswoman.com

Table of Contents

The Small Print

Privacy

The purpose of book promotion is to bring attention to books, authors, and publishers. The desire for publicity must be balanced with the need for privacy.

The information contained in these pages is for the personal use of the reader and may not be incorporated into publications, databases, or software programs, except in the form of brief excerpts or quotations with attribution for the purposes of review, without the written consent of Dan Poynter. Making copies of these pages or any portion for any purpose other than as stated is a violation of United States copyright laws.

Disclaimer

The Para Promotion Program and ParaPromotion.com and its employees and contractors are using their best efforts in preparing these pages and their services. The Para Promotion Program and ParaPromotion.com and its employees and contractors make no warranty of any kind, expressed or implied, with regard to the information and services supplied.

The intent of this book and other affiliated websites bearing the name "Dan Poynter" is to provide training, resources and opportunities to advance writing/self-publishing, the platform of books and other interests of Dan Poynter.

Limits of Liability

The Para Promotion Program and ParaPromotion.com and its employees and contractors shall not be liable in the event of incidental or consequential damages in connection with, or arising out of, the providing of the information and/or services offered here.

Trademarks

The Para Promotion Program and ParaPromotion.com and associated artwork are trademarks of Dan Poynter. All other product and brand names mentioned on this site are trademarks or registered trademarks of their respective owners.

Ownership

The Para Promotion Program and ParaPromotion.com are owned by Para Publishing, LLC.

Jurisdiction for legal compliance is California, USA.

Copyright

Copyright © 2000-2015 Dan Poynter and Para Publishing LLC. All Rights Reserved.

Content on this and other affiliated sites may be originated by other parties that hold respective copyrights.

Acknowledgments

I have often described Ellen as having a unique eye for quality. That description grew out of a time many years ago, when she showed me some of her work in before-and-after books. I was astonished: Her "after books" were the most attractive I had ever seen.

Ellen Reid

The original Book Shepherd, Ellen manages book production. She selects only the best subcontractors and brings them together to produce superior books of her design.

Ellen Reid creates books that are excellent in every way: books that not only have a vibrant cover, a title that grabs browsers, a sub-title that draws them to the back cover, and back cover text that compels to the sale... but one in which every element works synergistically with the others to supercharge the sales impact.

Ellen repeatedly confirms that she is the expert in excellence for independent publishing success.

Ghislain is an extraordinary type-setter/book designer. He has a unique ability to marry an attention-grabbing cover to a gorgeously designed text.

Ghislain Viau

For more than 20 years, he has specialized in creative book covers and interior layouts for small, independent publishers, and self-publishing authors.

Together Ellen and Ghislain produce award-winning books that make authors proud. This book is an example of their combined work.

Dan Poynter, Santa Barbara

Foreword

I learned everything about how to self-publish from Dan Poynter by reading his book *The Self-Publishing Manual* and taking his seminars at his home in Santa Barbara. He is the person who suggested I call myself a "Book Shepherd" and I have been honored to be one of the people he annointed with that mantle so many years ago. Since the late 1990s I have been helping authors start their own publishing companies and independently publish books of excellent quality. When our work was done, every single client had a book that could stand proudly next to those of the mainstream publishers and give authors a solid foundation for building their sales.

No matter how well these authors did, however, virtually everyone struggled with promoting their book. For years I resisted getting involved in book promotion. I wanted to put my energies into continually enhancing my skills and abilities to help authors get into print with a book they could be proud of.

Then I began sponsoring book contests to further support authors in being successful. I found out about Dan Poynter's Para Promotion Program and bought one to give as a prize for one of the contest winners. Then recently I realized the Para Promotion Program needed to be a printed book for authors and publishers to read and use. I suggested that Dan make it into a print book and an ebook and this is what you are reading now! My theory is that once you start seeing results, that will encourage you to move on to other promotional projects that may not have been your first choice. But even if you don't, there are enough simple and quickly accomplished tasks that will really assist you in reaching your target market and getting results

Once again, Dan Poynter has proven that he is, indeed, the Book Futurist!

Ellen Reid
www.indiebookexpert.com
www.indieexcellence.com
www.beverlyhillsbookawards.com (www.bhbookawards.com)
www.usaregionalexcellencebookawards.com (usareba.com)
ellen@indiebookexpert.com
iPhone: 805-403-5285

Preface

Book Publishers' Largest Complaint Answered

The author is at fault: Why don't authors promote their books?

Ask any publisher if authors promote their books and all will reply, "I wish mine did."

Publishers manufacture and distribute books. It is up to the authors to drive potential buyers to where the books are: stores, online, etc. The challenge is that most authors think the only way to promote books is on radio, television, and with autograph parties. And this promotion is a problem because most authors are introverts. They do not want to go out and promote. They want to stay home, be alone, and write.

Radio, television and autograph parties are not the only ways to promote books. There are many techniques introverted writers can use to get their books noticed while they stay at home. They can send out review copies, draft news releases, mention their book in their email signature, correspond with book bloggers (in their book's category), and much more.

In fact, today, introverts have an advantage: They like to spend time on social media. And social media is where the eyeballs are. Social media is huge while the millions of subgroups are categorized and easy to reach. For example, if you have a book on parachutes, it is easy to find skydivers who want to know about your book. Conversely, with search engines, it is easy for skydivers to find you, your subject and your book. Now authors can interact with their newfound "friends." This interaction is fun and easy because the authors get to discuss their favorite topic and they find they are treated as celebrities—because they wrote the book.

This book celebrates books and honors authors. Each of the book promotion assignments takes the author anywhere from 3 to 120 minutes to complete. The exercises not only gain attention for their book, it teaches them how to market their book—which they can use to launch their next book.

This program is not an overwhelming list of projects for authors, it is a collection of individual lessons.

Why Authors Find Book Promotion a Challenge

Writing a book is a solitary act, which may be why book writing appeals to introverts. Selling a book requires the outgoing gregariousness of extroverts and therein lays the conflict.

"It does not matter if you sell out to a large New York publisher or publish yourself, the author must do the promotion. The large five publishers in New York manufacture and distribute. They do not promote books."

So what is an author to do?

The major challenge is getting your book read, enjoyed, and recommended. That is called "benefiting from word of mouth."

Authors need help; they need to be shown how to let their potential readers know about their book. And the methods have to be fast, easy and cheap.

This book is designed to educate authors and bring attention to their books. The system starts with scores of tested ways to promote books. Authors discover how to promote their current book and their next and their next.

This book is for print books, ebooks and books available in other editions.

Any publicity you receive for one edition will help sell the other editions.

This program is so different you will be overjoyed. You will meet people in your "tribe," readers who love your subject as much as you do. You will be treated as a celebrity because you are the author of a book in their favorite field.

Introduction

Welcome to Dan Poynter's Para Promotion Program for authors.

Dan has often said: "Whether you sell out to a publisher or publish yourself, the author must do the promotion. Publishers do not promote books. It is up to you."

The Para Promotion Program is a strategy to successfully deliver your message to your "tribe." It guides you to potential clients who are as excited about your subject matter as you are. This is true target marketing.

The following pages are packed with book promotion opportunities. Some will take just a few minutes and some will take more time. We are breaking up the assignments so that you will not be overwhelmed with the work to do. I suggest completing one objective per week, but feel free to take your own pace.

Some of these assignments will be new to you and some will not—especially if you have been publishing for several years. If you have already joined this or built that, review what you have done, update the listing, and then congratulate yourself on completing the assignment.

Sometimes the project may seem difficult—not your kind of work—or you may just be too busy with other tasks. We have someone who will complete the project for you for a fee. The charge will depend on the project. But we urge you to learn from the lessons we send, rather than having someone else do them all for you. Gail Kearns is a book shepherd with more than 15 years of experience in books. She is a copywriter, ghostwriter, freelance book editor, and book publicist. Contact her at gmkea@aol.com, 805-898-2263. She lives in Santa Barbara.

Your mission is not to just complete each Opportunity; it is to make sure each one is done. To be successful, do not skip a project. Each one helps you to understand how to launch your marketing campaign.

Near the end of each Opportunity is a check-off area. Many of our clients like to print out, punch, and place these projects in a binder. Then they make notes on the assignments as they work through them. When finished, they date and check off the assignment as being completed.

These promotion opportunities will take time, but I promise you they will be worth it. The results will be encouraging and fun.

Now you are ready to start on your first book promotion assignment!

Book Promotion Opportunity #1

Join/Subscribe to Forums

Here is your initial project. Hopefully you are already subscribing to some of these forums. Subscribe to them all. Then spend some time on each Specific Genre Forum. Find the forums that match your book's subject matter.

Forums/Listservs offer free consulting and friendly networking. Ask any questions and you will receive numerous answers from people who have "been there."

You may sign up for instant feeds or daily digests. Receiving all the comments just once each day will reduce your email load.

Go to each group and subscribe. Study for a while and then contribute.

If you are not already a member of other Yahoo Groups, sign up before joining the forums on this list.

http://groups.yahoo.com/

a. Self-Publishing

This discussion forum is a community of authors and small presses interested or involved in publishing and marketing their own work and that of others. More than 3,000 members.

https://groups.yahoo.com/neo/groups/
Self-Publishing/info

b. The eBook Community

TeBC is the oldest, largest, and most respected forum for the general discussion of ebooks, the ebook industry, and related topics. Note that this forum has more than 3,700 subscribers and they love ebooks. Go to:

http://groups.yahoo.com/group/ebook-community/

Then see the button on the right of your screen to join this forum.

c. Print-On-Demand (POD)

This list is for published POD authors to exchange ideas of marketing, promotion, and sales of their books. Participants offer advice, suggestions, and support for authors of this new and exciting publishing industry. More than 1,200 members.

https://groups.yahoo.com/neo/groups/
Print-On-Demand/info

d. Print-On-Demand (POD)

This group is a business and marketing-oriented forum for print-on-demand and electronic publishers. (This list is NOT for first-time authors who want to publish a book using print-on-demand; there are other groups for that. This list is for publishers who intend to publish multiple titles and own their own ISBNs). More than 1,800 members.

https://groups.yahoo.com/neo/groups/
pod_publishers/info

e. Specific Genre Forums

The above forums are on book publishing.

For more forums on your book's specific subject, search Yahoo Groups at:

http://groups.yahoo.com/

For example, if you have a book on Arabian horses, search for forums on Arabian horses. Connect with a world of people who share your passion. You will be viewed as a celebrity on genre forums because you "wrote the book."

Join the forums that closely match the subject of your book. Your new friends will be sources of information for your revised edition and will ready buyers for your current edition.

Progress Record

Date & time started: _____

Date & time completed: _____

Book Promotion Opportunity #2

Google Alerts

Do you receive Google Alerts yet?

It is essential that you subscribe to Google Alerts. Google
Alerts is a free, electronic,
instant clipping service. With
them, you will find out:

1. The results of *our* efforts publicizing your book and
   books in general.

2. The results of *your* efforts promoting your individual
   book, in particular.

3. The latest news about your category/genre of book.
   When your book's title, your name, your company,
   or your subject is mentioned in a blog, website, news

article, or anywhere online, you will receive an alert (again, free). This is an easy way to keep current on your subject.

Dan Poynter finished his book on air travel. Then he realized he forgot to add "Air Travel" to his list on Google Alerts. Over the next five weeks, his book grew from 144 to 223 pages. The alerts from Google not only supplied additional information, but it was all brand new and up–to-date.

Alerts are specific and do not waste your time. They focus on your interests. Examples are science fiction, motorcycles, or relationships.

Fiction often revolves around an industry, geographic location, activity, etc. Add those keywords to your Google Alerts.

If you already subscribe to Google Alerts, review the keywords you want searched. See below for suggestions.

If you are not signed up for this free clipping service, please do it now. You will be amazed at what information comes to you.

Go to http://www.google.com/alerts

Set up your account and see the instructions at http://bit.ly/ok8zD5

The system will not take long to learn and will be well worth your effort.

Here are some search terms we suggest you enter:

> Your book's title
> Your name
> Your company's name
> eBook
> For example:
> "Para Promotion"
> "Global eBook Awards"
> "Dan Poynter"
> "Para Publishing"
> The category of your book (such as "Air Travel")

Where the term has more than one word, use quotation marks, such as "Air Travel." Otherwise you will be notified whenever the word "Air" or the word "Travel" appear online. In the example, you want only "Air Travel."

We ask you to sign up for "Para Promotion" so that you will receive notices of the promotion we are doing for you. Some of these are in the form of news releases distributed worldwide.

Please sign up for Goggle Alerts right now so you will be able to see what we are doing to promote your title.

Sign-up is essential. Your book deserves your attention.

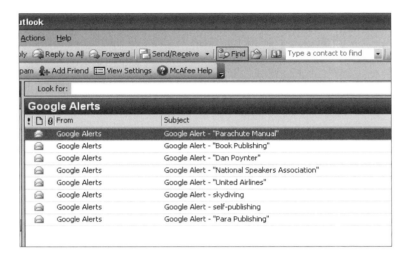

This research has a stimulating effect. Receiving Google Alerts each day will remind you of your project and make you come up with great ideas.

Progress Record

Date & time started: _____

Date & time completed: _____

Book Promotion Opportunity #3

Email Announcement to Your own Address Book

Draft a one-sheet book announcement. If you did a good job on your back cover sales copy, you can use most of it here. Don't forget to end with information on where the book can be found. Include your address, the exact URL on Amazon, and price.

Send this "brochure" to everyone in your email address book. Do not ask your contacts to purchase the book; instead, ask them for help. Be aware that while many might like you, they may not be interested in your book. If you ask them to buy a book, they are likely to delay action. Asking for help is different. Your friends want to help you. In fact, many will like to brag to their colleagues that they know a published author.

In the email message, type your own name in the To: line. Copy>Paste addresses from your address book into the Bcc: (blind copy) line. Don't give away any email addresses.

Many email systems have a message limit to combat spam. Gmail, for example, limits you to no more than two 99-address messages per day. Exceed those numbers and your email may be shut off until midnight.

Depending on the size of your address book, you may have to resend your message over a few days.

This is not spam since you are sending to people who know you and who have been added to your address book.

Ask your friends to help you by forwarding your announcement to anyone in their address book who might be interested in the book's subject.

Dan Poynter wrote a book titled *The Older Cat: Recognizing Decline and Extending Life.* He sent an announcement to everyone in his address book. He asked friends to forward the announcement to anyone they knew with an older cat.

Note, he did not request it to be passed along to "everyone," nor to "everyone with a cat," but just to people with an *older* cat.

This type of promotion is using "word-of-mouth" marketing and targeting the message.

The person receiving the message will recognize the name of the sender. They will be grateful that their friend was so thoughtful to send them information on a book with a subject that interests them.

Sending book announcements and asking your friends to help you spread the word is an example of book promotion that costs time but not money.

Progress Record

Date & time started: _____

Date & time completed: _____

Book Promotion Opportunity #4

Locating Reporters on Your Subject

Here is the easiest way to get media coverage for your book: when the journalist, editor, or producer has already decided to cover your particular subject and they're actively seeking people just like you to interview.

Reporters and other news writers often locate information sources through online services. By subscribing to these (free) listings, you can contribute to articles *when* they are being written.

Simply subscribe to the services below, read over the daily postings, and respond to the reporter or editor when you find a match with the subject matter of your book.

As an author of a book, you are a treasured resource who is quotable.

a. *Help A Reporter Out (HARO)*

Sign up at:

http://www.helpareporter.com/sources

http://www.facebook.com/HelpAReporter

Read about HARO at:

http://bit.ly/qTcTAR

Dan Poynter responded to a HARO request on taxes in New York. He relayed how shocked he was to find $53.00 in taxes, per night, added to his hotel bill after attending the 2010 BEA Book Fair. After the 2011 fair, *The New York Times* sent over a photographer and the result was a two-column story and a photo of him looking at his hotel bill in that prestigious paper.

b. *Reporter Connection*

Steve Harrison will send you subjects that editors and journalists are researching for articles. Sign up at:

http://www.reporterconnection.com/JoinNow/?11531

c. *PitchRate*

PitchRate gives you free and instant access to the media. By making it easy for you to connect with journalists in need of your expertise, PitchRate helps you land the kind of media coverage that boosts your exposure and catapults you and your business to the next level!

Sign up at:

http://www.pitchrate.com/

Progress Record
Date & time started: _____
Date & time completed: _____

Book Promotion Opportunity #5

Free eBook Glossary

Glossary of eBook Publishing Terms

See the glossary of ebook terminology in the FAQ at:
http://www.smashwords.com/about/supportfaq#glossary

Copy, print out, read, and save. You can't become an ebook expert until you learn the lingo. This free glossary will help.

Free eBook Glossary from eBook Friendly
http://ebookfriendly.com/ebooks-glossary-of-terms/

Progress Record
Date & time started: _____
Date & time completed: _____

Book Promotion
Opportunity #6

Draft and Send News Releases
on Your Book

To discover how easy and fun news releases are, start with local media. They love to run local news, especially about local residents.

Media includes newspapers, magazines, radio, TV, local tourist-oriented websites, and so on. Start your search using the Yellow Pages, and then go online.

Most of the media lists you compile will be genre-specific to your book. Local media are different. They are interested in you, the author. The only thing these media have in common is that they are local to you.

Make Google searches for your local zip codes + newspaper, magazine, radio, and television. You will be amazed at how many media outlets there are in your community. Add them to your list of local media.

Below is a news release outline. Just edit and send to:

a. Your local newspaper(s)

Go online to get their specific email addresses. Send the release to the "Local," "Community," or "Human Interest" section if your paper has one of them. Look further for a subsection for "Business" or "Books."

Most newspapers also publish websites. "Extra" material that can't fit on printed pages is often broadcast on websites. For an example of a local newspaper's website, see:

http://www.newspress.com/Top/Section/BUSINESS

Newspapers put their articles on wire services so your mention may be picked up by papers and other media outlets worldwide.

b. Local magazines

Do the same for local magazines. Look for a "Features," Personalities," or "Book" section. Again, start your list using the Yellow Pages and then search online.

For an example of a local magazine, see:

http://sbmag.com/category/feature

c. Local radio and TV stations

These are your next lists to compile.

Again, start your list using the Yellow Pages and then search online.

d. Local bookstores

Again, start your list with the Yellow Pages and then search online. Collect their email addresses.

For an example, make a Google search similar to Bookstore + "Santa Barbara."

e. Local tourist-oriented websites

Let them know that you are a member of the local author community by sending your news release to them.

f. Local online calendars

If you are having an event such as an autograph party, list the occasion on local online calendars.

Research online for calendars published by your local Chamber of Commerce and tourist bureaus.

Below is a news release outline:

Your "letterhead": Company name and logo

For Immediate Release . . .

Contact: [Author's name]
[Mobile phone #]
[Email address]

Headline in caps

LOCAL [AUTHOR] PUBLISHES
BOOK ON [SUBJECT]

Type a descriptive, clever, and catchy headline in capital letters and center it. Lure the editor to read more. Then space down four lines and get into the body of the release.

Opening

CITY, STATE - DATE – [Name of author] [Title of book] publishes book on [subject].

Issue or challenge

The lead paragraph is designed to invite the largest number of people to read the article. It must have broad appeal; make it interesting. The release should be *issue-oriented*; write about the *problem*, not the book. The release should begin by stating the problem and telling why this is an important subject. Make it provocative.

Numbers/statistics will help. For example, how many does this problem affect? Is it a work of fiction? If so, how many are reading this genre?

Development

Spend time on a second paragraph developing the message. Put the most interesting information first to keep the reader reading. Recite the most important items in descending order so that if some are cut from the end, the most important will remain. Provide interesting facts and statistics.

[Insert .jpg photo of the book's front cover]

How the book answers the question or solves the problem

Now move from a *what* to the *how* orientation. It is not necessary to dwell on the book. Anyone who finishes the article will be interested in the book. Then describe the contents of the book; mention it as a resource. Continue with some background on the topic and show why your book is unique, useful, and timely. Recite the benefits.

Author

Write a short paragraph about the author and tell why the author is an expert on the subject. Or what prompted you to be interested in this genre of fiction.

[Insert .jpg photo of the author]

Ordering information

List the price and say that the book is available from the publisher, in local stores, Amazon, or wherever. List your website URL and telephone number so the reader will know where to send the money. Most orders will go through Amazon.

End the release with the newspaper termination sign:

###

Email this release to local media outlets. Later we will show you how to send it to media worldwide.

If you signed up for Google Alerts as we suggested earlier in this Promo Program, you will see results from sending news releases to local media very soon.

Progress Record
Date & time started: _____
Date & time completed: _____

Book Promotion Opportunity #7

List of Book Reviewers

Request reviews at Amazon, B&N.com, and other review opportunities.

A Fabulous List of Reviewers

Reviews sell books. Reviews make your book appear important. Solicit as many reviews as possible.

Reviews are the most effective and least expensive form of book promotion—far cheaper than an ad.

Here is a targeted list of reviewers—with the categories they want. This list is constantly updated. Send books only when your book matches the reviewer's liking. Match your book to their stated preferences. On the other hand, when in doubt, ship it out.

http://www.bookrevieweryellowpages.com/
reviewer-list.html

Scroll down to the alphabetical list.

Progress Record
Date & time started: _____
Date & time completed: _____

Book Promotion Opportunity #8

Setting Up Your Book's Contact List

Eyeballs have moved from print to online. Advertisers know this. They have moved their money to the Internet.

You should send review copies to book bloggers, websites, forum leaders, and other opinion-molders in your book's category. Start with the book bloggers.

Book bloggers are the new book reviewers. And there are 152,000,000 blogs on the Internet.

Review copies should be sent to book bloggers and subject matter expert bloggers who focus on **your book's category**. For example, books on leadership should only go to blogs on leadership.

We've heard stories of book sales that have taken off

after mentions by bloggers. But how can you make this phenomenon work for your book?

There are bloggers, bloggers on subjects, and book bloggers. All are valuable to you, but the book bloggers are the best because they write about books and are book category-oriented. Few bloggers read and comment on anything else.

Most of the book bloggers are female, young, a high percentage are moms, and most read and write about Young Adult (YA) books. No surprise. But many focus on historical fiction, women's studies, and all the other genres.

So how do you find bloggers who want to be notified about your books? Make a Google search for "book blogger directory." Better yet, narrow your search. If you have a book on horses, search for "horse book blogger directory." You will be amazed at what you find.

Start with a network of nearly 2,000 book bloggers and book reviewers at:

http://bookblogs.ning.com/group/dedicatedbookreviewers
and http://www.google.com/blogsearch

Now the work begins: finding bloggers' names, email addresses, and other contact details. Many do not even list their last name on their blog sites. But this work is well worth the effort. You will be contacting your new friends over and over.

Remember, these aren't just any bloggers; they are those that love books in your category (such as horses). They are members of your tribe. They love the same subject you love.

Book bloggers are the new reviewers. Blogers are influential in their fields. Reviews and mentions sell books. Make up your list of bloggers now.

You may want to enter the contact information into an Excel spreadsheet. That way you can continue to add further contact details, such as street addresses, and the list becomes sortable. It is easy to add to and it's easy to pull off the postal and email addresses for individual and group mailings.

The list you assemble will be a valuable company asset and will be used over and over again.

The columns may be labeled: category, business name, contact name, email, website, blog, address (as in street address), city, state, ZIP code/country, telephone, mobile phone, fax, project manager, and comments.

The category column is where you list whether it is a blog, forum, website, print magazine, and so on.

The list you assemble will be focused on your category. General review publications are not likely to reach a large number of people interested in your subject. You will use this list to send review copies, news releases, and other announcements on your subject and book.

Assembling this list will be both valuable and fun. You will discover people all over the world interested in your subject and eager to know about your book.

Progress Record
Date & time started: _____
Date & time completed: _____

Book Promotion Opportunity #9

List of Book Reviewers

*T*he *Book Reviewer Yellow Pages* lists ONLY book reviewers that will accept self-published and POD books. No more time wasted trying to get book reviews, only to hear, "Oh, we don't accept POD." All of the book reviewers listed are NO-FEE reviewers.

Each listing details the individual book reviewer's contact information, accepted genres, and submission guidelines.

In addition, all the reviewers are rated for quality and influence. The longer a reviewer has been posting reviews, and the more followers they have, the higher the site ranking.

Get this book. Send review copies to reviewers that like your book's category. Printed books will be reviewed more often than ebooks.

Progress Record
Date & time started: _____
Date & time completed: _____

Book Promotion Opportunity #10

Amazon Reviews

Amazon reviews are the most powerful reviews because they are written by several different readers, not just a single book critic. And these **amazon**.com readers actually bought and read the book.

Here are three ways to build your Amazon reviews:

1. Review Similar Books at Amazon

Think, if someone were to buy and read another book, would they be likely to want to know about your book? Look over similar titles and select the ones you like best. Review the books, give them five stars, and sign your review with your name and your book's title. That puts your name and your book's title on their page.

Note, while your name and book title may be above the review, they could be overlooked there.

2. Get Friends to Review Your Book

Draft some helpful copy for them. It will be easier for them to edit your draft than to try to be creative starting from scratch.

3. Get Friends to Review Similar Books and Recommend Your Book.

Ask them to review similar books, rave about them, give them five stars, and then suggest that anyone liking this book might also be interested in your book (list the title and author).

People favor certain types of books. I like creatively-written, accurate, historical fiction. The challenge is that my favorite authors do not write as quickly as I read. So, I am always searching for new authors. Consequently, I read the Amazon reviews looking for recommendations.

It is rumored that once your reviews amount to 25, Amazon takes notice and does free publicity for you. One promotion might be their mailings saying to clients that "you've read this book, so you might be interested in these books in the same category."

Invest your time and build your collection of Amazon reviews.

And once you have drafted copy, change the headline and a few words and post the new draft at B&N.com.

Progress Record
Date & time started: _____
Date & time completed: _____

Book Promotion Opportunity #11

A List of Book Reviewer Websites

Reviews sell books. Reviews make your book appear important. Solicit as many reviews as possible. Reviews are the least expensive form of book promotion; cheaper than an ad.

http://www.webring.org/hub/bookreviews

Click on an image of one of the book review sites. Look for reviewers who like your genre. Go to the bottom of the page. Run your cursor over the name and send an email asking if they would like your book in paper or electronic form. If paper, request a postal address.

Close that window and click on:

Show more member sites on this page!

Repeat.

Go up to the search box and type in your book's category. Click on "All Rings." Search around the site to make sure you have found every possible match for your book.

Add websites and blogs to your collection of promotional contacts.

Progress Record
Date & time started: _____
Date & time completed: _____

Book Promotion Opportunity #12

Another List of Book Reviewers

Gather as many specific, targeted potential reviewers as possible. For example, not "animals," not "horses," but specifically "quarter horses." Some people love quarter horses while most people do not even care about horses. Those who love quarter horses probably do not read about Arabian horses. Be specific. Talk to your "tribe."

Here is a list of reviewers of specific-category nonfiction books. If your book is fiction, do not pass this up. Your book is fiction and it is ABOUT a category. Using the above example, your work of fiction may be about a horse, so look for reviewers that concentrate on (nonfiction) horses.

http://www.ebookcrossroads.com/

Look through the categories they list and pick out matches with your book's category. Most list postal addresses.

Send a printed book. If you are not sure of the match of your book with their stated wants, send the book. Your book is its own ambassador; it speaks for itself—loudly. When in doubt, send it out.

Search around the site for more matches with your book.

By the way, be patient. Reviews take time—3 months to 3 years. The review copies must be (leisurely) read, the review written, and the review posted.

Occasionally, the reviewer may not like your book enough to give it 5 stars. They may decide not to review it than to down-rate it. In this case, no review is better than a negative review.

Progress Record
Date & time started: _____
Date & time completed: _____

Book Promotion Opportunity #13

Get Listed in Wikipedia

Having your bio on Wikipedia has become very important for both authors and publishers. Many people in the media and business feel that if you have not qualified to be in Wikipedia, you are not important.

To be listed in Wikipedia, you can't just fill out a form. In fact, it is difficult to be accepted if you send in your own listing. Wikipedia is very particular. They want every entry in a bio to be substantiated.

Look at some pages of authors. Note the footnotes at the bottom. Every fact is referenced. For example, see:

http://en.wikipedia.org/wiki/Dan_Poynter.

The easiest way to get into Wikipedia is to draft your own page (with documented references) and then have it cleaned up and submitted by someone who has a good track record with Wikipedia—someone they trust.

One such person is Andy Davis. Contact him at AndyWDavis@Yahoo.com for pricing and details. Expect the cost to be less than $200, depending on length and complexity.

Progress Record

Date & time started: _____

Date & time completed: _____

Book Promotion
Opportunity #14

Email Signature

If you currently have a signature at the end of your emails—congratulations. You are special because more than 92% of authors and publishers do not.

An email signature or .sig is verbiage automatically appended to the end of each email you send. It tells who you are, what you do, and how to find you. If you have a business card, you need a signature.

.sigs are the least expensive (free) and most effective promotion you can do. Once set up, they are automatic.

If you already have a signature, your assignment this week is to improve it. Review it, clean it up, and add photos of yourself and your book cover. For the rest of you, it is time to set up one.

For example, here is the .sig I am using this week. Use it as a guide.

When I am traveling, my messages tend to be short. Thank you for your understanding.

~~~~~~

Dan Poynter, Author (127 Books), Publisher (Since 1969), Speaker (CSP).

Para Publishing LLC, PO Box 8206, Santa Barbara, CA 93118-8206, USA.

Bus: +1-805-968-7277; Mob: +1-805-448-9009

DanPoynter@ParaPublishing.com

http://ParaPublishing.com

http://GlobaleBookAwards.com

http://ParaPromotion.com

http://ParaShelf.com

Follow me: http://www.Twitter.com/DanPoynter

See me: http://www.youtube.com/watch?v=mWl0fnBu7bs

Whether you use Outlook, Mac Mail or some other program, click on Help and type in "signature" or "use signatures in mail." Instructions on creating a .sig will appear.

Your first attempt at a .sig might take 15 minutes. Changes can be made in a minute or two.

As an author and/or a publisher, you are in business. You will get more business if people know who you are, what you do, and how to contact you. A .sig is the least expensive, easiest, and least time-consuming promotion project you can do.

Progress Record
Date & time started: _____
Date & time completed: _____

Book Promotion Opportunity #15

Artwork: Logos, Mastheads, Banners, and More

A company needs a logo: an instantly-recognizable piece of art that reminds people of you, your company, and your book. Your website, blog, or newsletter need a masthead. A good masthead makes you look stable and established.

To find artists who can design you logo and other art, see:
http://parapublishing.com/sites/para/
resources/supplier.cfm#6

Logos

Here are examples of logos Sean Somics has created for us. This young man is a college student holding down two part-time jobs.

Mastheads

Banners

Receive more than 50 tips and tricks
as well as new and classic methods
to increase book sales all year long

Hire an Artist

Logos, mastheads, and banners are a good investment. We found Sean Somics last year. He is a talented college student with low hourly fees. You will be amazed at what he can do for very little cost. See his website and contact him. Examples of some of the work he has done for us are above.

http://somicsdesigns.com

+1-805-451-8794

Progress Record
Date & time started: _____
Date & time completed: _____

Book Promotion Opportunity #16

Publishing Poynters Marketplace: Asking for Book Reviews

Reviews at online bookstores sell books. Here is a way to ask fellow authors and publishers to review your book at Amazon.com, B&N.com, and other websites.

In *Publishing Poynters Marketplace*, you may post requests for *stories* for the book you are writing, and offer *review* copies to other authors and publishers willing to post a review at Amazon.com and B&N.com. There is no charge for listing your book.

Look over a current issue of the ezine by going to:
http://parapublishing.com/sites/para/
resources/newsletter.cfm

Scroll down and click on the most recent issue of the *Marketplace*.

Read down the ezine and then focus on the D. ParaReviews section. See the submission instructions.

You must be willing to send a book and promotional materials (review book package) to readers of *Publishing Poynters Marketplace* who contact you (usually 5 to 10 requests).

Include the number of pages in your description, and for children's books, list the age level for which the book is written. Make sure the book is already listed at Amazon.com.

Just send your request and description to DanPoynter@ ParaPublishing.com. Describe the book in a few words. Potential reviewers only need enough information to see if they have expertise and an interest in your category. Include a .jpg image of the cover.

Supply full contact information, including your email address. Write the draft as it should appear so that we do not have to do more than copy/paste. Put "Review Wanted" in the subject line so we will know this is not just another book announcement (we get a lot of them). Don't forget to be patient.

The *Publishing Poynters Marketplace* makes getting reviews easy and it is free.

Progress Record

Date & time started: _____

Date & time completed: _____

Book Promotion
Opportunity #17

Make a Book Trailer

Book trailers are the latest promotion rage. So many books have trailers today that if you do not have one, people wonder if your book is important.

Book trailers should be posted at YouTube. Not only will they be seen by people you send to the specific URL, but surfers and web searchers  will run across it. Your book wins either way.

See book trailers made by Joseph Dowdy for books entered in the Global eBook Awards at:

http://goo.gl/IKq3Z

Fabulous audio and video make your book stand out.

Dowdy will post your 30-second video at YouTube for you. The YouTube URL may be referenced in your email signature, on your website, in your blog, in your promotion mailings, on your Facebook page, and so on.

If your book is entered in the Global eBook Awards, the trailer can be made for $149. Custom trailers for other books are $199. Contact Joseph Dowdy at +1-805-742-4631 joseph@meshmarketer.com and get more information on his trailer work at:

http://meshmarketer.com/social-media/
book-and-ebook-trailers/

Progress Record
Date & time started: _____
Date & time completed: _____

Book Promotion
Opportunity #18

Success Stories

Listing your books on other websites not only gets them more exposure, but your Search Engine Optimization (SEO) is rated higher when you list your website's URL. Here is a site where you can list your book(s):

You may list your book along with your email address and website URL to direct orders and inquiries back to you. Click the below link to list your book. The listing is FREE.

http://parapub.com/sites/para/resources/success_list.cfm

Then, select one of the below subjects:

- Antiques / Collectibles
- Architecture
- Art
- Aviation
- Biography / Autobiography / Letters
- Business / Economics / Finance

- Children's Books
- Computer / Web / eCommerce
- Cooking / Food
- Craft & Hobbies
- Current Affairs
- Dance
- Drama
- Education
- Family / Child Care / Relationships
- Fiction / Literature
- Foreign Language Instruction and Reference
- Games
- Gardening & Horticulture
- Health / Fitness
- History
- Home Improvement & Construction
- How To
- Humor
- Inspiration
- Language Arts
- Law
- Literary Criticism & Essays
- Mathematics
- Medical / Nursing / Home Care
- Music
- Nature & Natural History
- New Age / Occultism / Parapsycholog
- Parenting
- Performing Arts
- Pets / Animals
- Philosophy
- Photography
- Poetry
- Political Science & Government
- Psychology / Psychiatry
- Publishing
- Real Estate / Homes
- Reference
- Relationships
- Science
- Self-Development
- Self-Improvement / Self-Help
- Social Sciences
- Spiritual / Religion / Bibles

- Sports / Recreation
- Study Aids
- Technology & Industrial Arts
- Transportation
- Travel & Travel Guides
- True Crime
- Writing

Progress Record
Date & time started: _____
Date & time completed: _____

Book Promotion Opportunity #19

Sizzle Reel

Sizzle reels were originally created to interest Hollywood producers, directors, and others in film ideas. They are fast-moving, to-the-point, exciting, and short. They are a videoed "elevator speech."

A sizzle reel is also known as a demo reel, a public relations video, and a promo, as well as about twenty other names. This is a short video, usually no more than three minutes in length that is used to get a message across about your business's brand.

A sizzle reel will make your book come alive visually and separate you from the pack.

Silver Screen Sizzles will take your book and turn it into a one- to two-minute sizzle reel, synthesizing your idea into a visually dynamic message. Sizzle reels can be referenced in emails, newsletters, blogs, and on websites. They are easily sent to publishers, agents, motion picture/ television, and talk show producers, speaker's bureaus, or used for corporate presentations. The sizzle reel will give you a leg up on the competition.

Silver Screen Sizzles is the creation of producer, writer, and director Rocky Lang and director Scott Barker.

Rocky Lang, a thirty-year veteran of the motion picture, television, and publishing world, has produced movies such as Ridley Scott's *White Squall* and the Emmy Award-winning *Titanic*, and is the author of five published books.

Scott Barker oversees all production. Scott just completed directing his first feature film *Spinners*, and has edited, shot, and directed scores of trailers and sizzle reels.

Their philosophy is to integrate new media and contemporary marketing strategies to help attract eyeballs and buyers to the book.

Contact:
Silver Screen Sizzles
Rocky Lang
rocky@silverscreensizzles.com
+1-818-203-8385, +1-818-993-5255

Their examples will amaze you:

http://www.youtube.com/watch?v=mWl0fnBu7bs
http://silverscreensizzles.com/SSS/Book_Sizzles.html

Progress Record

Date & time started: _____

Date & time completed: _____

Book Promotion Opportunity #20

Smashwords: Easy Review eBook Distribution

Most authors and publishers send ebooks to reviewers in PDF format—and that is the problem. Reviewers read a lot and often while on the move. They want to read on their iPad, iPhone, Kindle, or other electronic eReader. So, there is a greater chance a reviewer will select your book for review if it is available in the format they like. And chances are they will read your book sooner.

Smashwords can make your book available in eight formats at NO CHARGE: PDF, MobiPocket, Palm, ePub, Sony, Kindle, among other formats.

And when a reviewer downloads your book, Smashwords sends you a notice just as they do when your ebook is purchased.

Once your book is uploaded into the Smashwords system at http://Smashwords.com, you are ready.

Log on to Smashwords and locate your book. Look to the right side and click on *Manage this book's coupon.*

Smashwords Coupon Code Manager

This page allows you to assign coupon codes to books that you can then share with reviewers. Reviewers enter the code prior to completing their checkout to receive a 100% discount. Click on Generate Coupon and copy the code.

You can limit the use of the coupon code by setting an expiration date or changing it at any time.

Title	Base Price	Coupon Code	Coupon Price	Coupon Created	Coupon Starts	Coupon Expires	Actions
Air Travel Handbook	$4.97	~~BA47X~~	$0.00 (~100% off)	11/05/11	Immediately	11/14/11	Generate Coupon

Set up a coupon code for your book and then offer your book for review to book bloggers on your book's subject/category.

The Global eBook Awards uses Smashwords to supply ebook review copies to the judges. Judges can easily retrieve the ebook formats of their choice.

If you're ready to get started with Smashwords, go to: http://Smashwords.com

Progress Record

Date & time started: _____

Date & time completed: _____

Book Promotion
Opportunity #21

Pocket-Sized Book Brochures:
Book Promotion Cards

There is no longer a need to design, print, and mail brochures on books. Design is still needed, but print has been replaced by our websites and blogs, while email has replaced postal mail.

That being said, there are times when we wish we had something more direct and explanatory to hand out at functions besides business cards. Business cards remind people about us, while book promotion cards tell about our product or service.

Book promo cards are larger than business cards, but they are still pocket-sized. Typically, they display the book's cover, a photo of the author, a description of the book, and URLs where the book can be purchased.

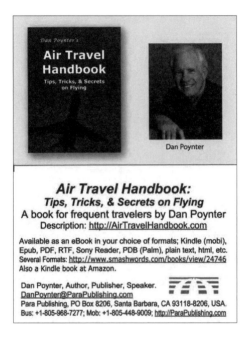

Imagine a pocket-sized card measuring 2.75 x 4.25 announcing and describing your book. Not a typical business card but a small brochure you can hand to people—and they can slip it into a pocket.

These unique cards are the brainchild of author Dan Poynter and cover artist Robert Howard. Rough out what you want and Robert will design your cards, then have them printed and delivered directly to you.

The cards are printed in color on both sides (4/4) on heavy 14-pt. gloss (slick) stock.

The cost is unbelievably low at $200 for 2,500 gorgeous promotion cards plus artwork and shipping.

Contact Robert Howard at:
>rhdesign@q.com
>+1-970-225-0083
>http://www.BookGraphics.com
>rHoward@BookGraphics.com

Progress Record

Date & time started: _____

Date & time completed: _____

Book Promotion
Opportunity #22

Drafting Book Sales
Copy That Sells

Some of you may say, "Dan has been talking about the importance of back cover sales copy for a long time. I know all about it." Yes, but few authors follow instructions and produce effective sales copy. We know because we receive several books each week from authors who have used *The Self-Publishing Manual* to guide them in publishing.

Most printed book back covers do not adequately describe the contents of the book. The outside does not sell the inside.

While ebooks do not normally have back covers, they do need hard-punching sales copy to describe them. This book cover worksheet can be used to draft the ebook description for your website, blog, listings at Amazon and B&N.com, in news releases, and more. Write it once and use it over and over.

Everyone Judges a Book by its Cover

And what you can do about it?

Think about it: No one reads the book before he or she makes a buying decision. Consumers do not read the book in the store or online. Sales reps only carry book covers and jackets to show store buyers, while wholesalers and distributors say, "Just send us the cover copy." All buying decisions are made on the illustration/design and the sales copy on the outside of the book. Yes, packaging is everything.

Each year, the U.S. industry spends more than $50 billion on package design. Now, that is not $50 billion for the packages and certainly not for the contents. That money is for the *design* of the packages. Packages prompt buyers to reach for the product whether it is panty hose, cornflakes, or hair spray.

Stores have tens of thousands of books being displayed spine out. With all this congestion, it is hard to get attention. Initially, all a potential buyer sees is the book's spine. If the browser takes it down, he or she will gaze at the cover for about four seconds and then flip it over to read the back cover. On average, he or she will spend just seven seconds here, so the trick is to keep them reading longer. Your copy has to be punchy and benefit-laden; it has to speak to the potential buyer.

Your book cover designer will lay out the package and incorporate the illustration, put it all in a file, and send it to your printer, but you must draft the sales copy. This book cover worksheet will take you step by step through the sales copy draft process. Use your computer so you will be able to move the copy around once entered.

Drafting ad copy is hard work. Ad copy writers—people who write ads for a living—need to stimulate their imagination. Most of them study the field constantly. When they see an element of an ad they like in a magazine or online, they will pull it out, circle the good part, and put it in a "swipe file." When they are commissioned to write an ad, they will go through the swipe file looking for ideas. You can use the same stimulating procedure, but there is an easier, more direct way to do it.

Look for four to six other books at Amazon that are very close to your book. Think to yourself, *If someone were to buy that book, would they be a good candidate to buy my book?*

Print out the multiple pages. Highlight the buzzwords and good book descriptions. Now, spread out the pages and draft your sales copy. All the good, descriptive sales copy is in front of you. The highlighting will stimulate your copywriting imagination and make the drafting easy.

Here are explanations for each area of the outline.

A. Front Cover

Select a working title and subtitle. Keep the title short and make the subtitle descriptive.

List the most important person in your field (association or industry) for the foreword (and please note the proper spelling of *foreword*). You will try to get them to pen the foreword later.

B. Spine

Stack the title on the spine so it will read more easily on the shelf. Use a bold, san-serif, vertically-legged typeface such as Arial Black, bolded.

C. Back Cover

1. **Category.** Visit a bookstore and check the shelf where your book will be displayed. Note the categories on the books and the shelves. Listing the category on the back cover of your book will insure your book will be easy to find—because the bookshop personnel will place it on the right shelf.

2. Now you need an arresting **headline** addressed to potential buyers. You want them to relate to the book and find themselves in it. Do not repeat the title here; do not bore the potential buyer. You have already "said it" on the front. Use an alternate approach. For example, *The*

Self-Publishing Manual's back cover headline is *Why Not Publish Yourself?*

3. **Sales copy.** Concisely (two to four sentences) state what the book is about. What will the reader gain by reading this book?

4. **Bulleted promises or benefits.** Promise to make readers better at what they do. Pledge health, wealth, entertainment, or a better life. Be specific. Focus on who your audience is and what they want. Think about who you are talking to and what they are going to get from the book.

   You will discover:
   - (benefit)
   - (benefit)
   - (benefit)
   - (benefit)

5. **Testimonials and endorsements.** Dream up three different endorsements from people you would *like* to quote. If *This book changed my diplomatic strategy.*—Colin Powell, would look good, *try* it. Use *names* or *titles* recognizable in your field—sources that might impress potential buyers. This is just a draft; dress it up. You will secure some of these quotations later.

6. Show the **author** is the ultimate authority on the subject. Just two or three sentences will do.

7. End with a **sales closer** in bold type. Ask the book-browser to buy the book. Use something like *This book has enabled thousands to ... and it will show you the way too.*

8. **Price.** Bookstores like a price on the book. The price is a turn-off to potential buyers, so place it at the end of the sales copy. Never locate the price at the top of the back cover. If this is a hardcover book, place the price at the top of the front flap.

9. **Bar code** with International Standard Book Number (ISBN). The bar code on a book identifies the ISBN, which in turn identifies the publisher, title, author, and edition (hardcover, etc.). Make room for, but do not worry about, the bar code and ISBN just now.

Your **title**, **subtitle**, back cover **headline**, and **benefits** may be swapped. Once you have them written down, you may wish to move some of them around. Perhaps one of your benefits would be a better subtitle.

Most back cover copy is weak and uninspiring. The title is repeated and then is followed by several quotations and a bar code and that's it! Haphazard copy is the sign of a lazy (and maybe inexperienced) copywriter. This lack of effective competition on the shelf gives the smaller publisher an upper hand.

Book cover illustrations and design have improved tremendously over the past 30 years. Author/publishers used to spend all their efforts on the text and the cover became an afterthought. Some publishers remember it was Robert Howard who brought bright, insightful, relevant, remarkable covers to the industry. There are many great cover designers today and it was Robert Howard who started it all.

For a list of cover artists, see:

http://parapub.com/sites/para/resources/supplier.cfm#6

Each has a different style. Visit their websites and look for a style that will attract your audience.

A good cover artist will read through your book and create a cover that will reflect the message of the text. The cover and text should match.

Use your back cover copy in your brochures, website, blog, Amazon listing, and so on. Just change it slightly to fit their format.

Years ago, we said, "Write your ad before you write your book." This was to help you focus on whom you were writing to and what you were going to give them. Then we realized the most important ad you will ever write is your back cover copy. Now we say: "Write your cover copy before you write your book."

Packages sell products and covers sell books. Give your books the opportunity in the marketplace they deserve. Package your text to quickly tell the idle browser what is inside.

See the paint-by-the-numbers instructions on how to write the sales copy and lay out your covers. Follow this outline; make your cover sell your book. Download this document and fill it in.

http://bit.ly/vX4Voq

Progress Record

Date & time started: _____

Date & time completed: _____

Book Promotion Opportunity #23

Discover Public Relations:
Subscribe to The Publicity Hound

Advertising costs money.

Publicity is free.

People read editorial copy.

They are skeptical of, and usually skip, advertising copy.

Publicity expert Joan Stewart shows you how  to use free publicity to establish your credibility, enhance your reputation, position yourself as an expert, sell more products and services, promote a favorite cause or issue, and position your company as an employer of choice.

Generate thousands of dollars in FREE PUBLICITY for your book, service, cause, or issue by subscribing to the FREE email newsletter "The Publicity Hound's Tips of the

Week." It's delivered every Tuesday and is loaded with tips, tricks and tools, case studies, and advice on how to work with the media.

Sign up for Joan's free newsletter. Do it now.
http://www.publicityhound.com/

Progress Record
Date & time started: _____
Date & time completed: _____

Book Promotion
Opportunity #24

Selling Books in Quantity—
Premium Sales

Premiums are products that are given away or sold at a discount to promote business. *Premiums* may be given away by a store or other business to attract customers while *incentives* are given to sales people as prizes for achieving sales goals. (An *ad specialty* is an imprinted product, such as a pen or key chain, that is given away.)

Premiums are often books.

The premium/incentive market is a $20 billion per year business. Books are in eighth place with $500 million in sales. According to *Potentials in Marketing* magazine, 16.8% of the companies using premiums use books. Books make especially good premiums and incentives, as printing a special cover may customize them and because they are held in higher esteem than some other premium trinkets. In fact, in some areas, regulated industries, such as banks, are prohibited from giving away certain items or the value of the items they may consider is limited.

Look for a company with products or services that closely match the book's subject matter. If your book covers a regional topic, try local businesses. Small quantities of books may be rubber-stamped with "Compliments of Valley National Bank," as an example. If you cover a subject with wider appeal, such as a book on beer can collecting, contact the beer, aluminum, steel, can, and packaging companies. Such a book would make an ideal corporate gift or might be worked into a promotion. A tour guidebook might be sold to a hotel chain.

(Letterhead)

February 31, 2012

Valley National Bank
George P. Moneybags, Vice President
State and Victoria Streets
Santa Barbara, CA 93000

Dear Mr. Moneybags:

Here is an exciting traffic-building premium idea for your bank: *Santa Barbara Highlights and History.*

This book capitalizes on Santa Barbarans' love for their city (see the descriptive brochure enclosed). This is an ideal way for Valley National to identify with its community. Everyone will want a copy.

We are offering you a special "private label" premium edition for your company's exclusive use within your industry. The book sells for $9.95 in stores, but we can offer you a 50% discount or more for a volume purchase (see the enclosed Dealer Bulletin listing prices). For orders of 1,000 or more, timed with our regular printings, we can offer your company a "with compliments" byline on the back cover for just an $80 artwork charge. For a $750 art charge, we could even put a picture of the bank on the back cover in full color.

If you would like to consider this book as a premium, we will be happy to drop by. Please write or call me today.

Sincerely,

AAPEX PUBLISHING

Henry M. Goodfellow
Marketing Manager

HMG/ms
Enclosures: Brochure, Dealer Bulletin

Judy Dugan was working in a graphic arts shop when the first edition of *The Self-Publishing Manual* was being typeset. As she pasted up the pages, she read the book and became increasingly interested. She had been toying with two manuscripts for years. She began asking the author all sorts of questions about the possibilities for her book. One problem she had was a lack of money to invest.

The author noticed that Valley National Bank was moving into a building in downtown Santa Barbara. He explained that they were a prime candidate for a regional book, as it would tie the out-of-town bank to the local community. A premium could be used to lure potential patrons into the bank.

In two short visits, she walked out with a purchase order for 5,000 copies in softcover and 1,000 copies in hardcover. She was paid one-half on signing and one-half on delivery at full list price. The money allowed her to print 11,000 books, so she could serve the local tourist market with her 5,000 copies.

The bank's copies had special back cover printing: "Compliments of ..." and the bank advertised in newspapers, on radio, and television. They invited people to come into the bank for a free autographed copy of the book. They set Judy up with a table and a sign, and she spent the week greeting people and signing her name.

Here is a directory of premium users:

Directory of Premium, Incentive and Travel Buyers
Salesman's Guide, Inc.
http://www.TheSalesmansGuide.com
http://bit.ly/rCYYeN

And some trade shows:
Sales Marketing Network
http://www.enterpriseengagement.org/
rewards/resources/events/

Promotional Products Association International
http://www.ppai.org

Premium orders are large, usually 1,000 or more books, and the customer may ask for 60% off. But ask what their budget for this promotion is before you quote a price. Such a discount can be justified for a large order that eliminates the problems of financing, storage, and individual shipping. A typical premium discount schedule might look like this:

Number of copies	Discounts
25-99	20%
100-499	40%
500-999	50%
1,000-14,999	60%
15,000 & up	Cost of printing plus 10% of list price

Plan your covers to leave a blank area for personalization such as a company logo. Offer companies short-run digital printing with their logo on the cover, a letter from the president inside, and so on. See our special report *Buying Book Printing.*

In larger companies, approach the "brand manager."

Ask for a purchase order with a 50% deposit stating that the order is non-cancelable, the books are non-returnable, and the freight is "collect."

If you can strike some premium deals before going to (or back to) press, you may increase your press run and achieve a lower per-unit printing cost. Early sales are also a great help in paying the first printing bill. Be prepared to do a lot of legwork. Premium sales are tough and time-consuming, but the payoff is big.

Do not forget to capitalize on a premium sale. For example, you might use "Official Recipe Book of the Pillsbury Company" or "Recommended by Radio Shack." Premium deals are not just sales; they are also endorsements.

Large Sales Take More Time

It is easier and quicker to sell an individual a single book than it is to sell a company a whole program. But larger numbers are often worth the effort and the wait.

In 1981, Dan Poynter wrote the first book on word processing. There were other books on office automation that referenced word processing, but none devoted solely to the subject, and interest was about to explode. He was contacted by the Xerox Corporation to write a book on their new 9700 laser-printing machine. Instead, he persuaded Xerox to set the type for *Word Processors and Information Processing* and to buy 1,000 copies so the sales reps could use them as examples of what the 9700 could deliver. As a bonus, Xerox gave him thousands of dollars' worth of computer equipment.

The problem was that a few weeks were lost in making the sale, and then months were lost working with the large company during typesetting. Another book appeared on word processing just after *Word Processors and Information Processing* hit the stores. *Word Processors* was still first, but it soon had competition instead of a clear field. The Xerox deal was a coup and an endorsement, but working with a large company delayed publication and hurt the book's market. Consider smaller markets when going this route.

You can also hire a rep to sell your book as a premium. Contact Brian Jud.

http://www.BookMarketingWorks.com
800-562-4357, 860-675-1344
BrianJud@bookmarketing.com

Progress Record

Date & time started: _____

Date & time completed: _____

Book Promotion Opportunity #25

Stats on Book Sales— Amazon Author Central & BookScan

How and where is your book selling? Knowing what type of **amazon** Author Central reader or outlet is buying will help you focus your promotional efforts most efficiently in the right places.

Sign up for Amazon's Author Central and use BookScan to track your sales from the bookstores and other book outlets. Subscription to BookScan is normally expensive. Amazon makes your numbers available to you free.

Sign in/sign up at:

https://authorcentral.amazon.com/gp/login.html

Add to your profile and confirm your list of books.

Click on the Help Topics > Your Books > Sales Information or click on this link:

http://bit.ly/uf3tyl

You will get timely sales data free. Nielsen BookScan collects the majority of point-of-sale data each week from more than 10,000 retailers, both online and off—some 75% of the industry.

This BookScan feature of Amazon Central will help you track your sales and evaluate your book promotion progress.

Progress Record
Date & time started: _____
Date & time completed: _____

Book Promotion Opportunity #26

Subscribe to the Smashwords Blog

Mark Coker shares the latest ebook information in his blog. You can subscribe for free or read it online. You may receive the blog via RSS reader or receive individual new blog postings via email.

http://blog.smashwords.com

See the delivery choice on the right-hand side of your screen.

Or read *Smashwords News* at:

http://globalebookawards.com

http://parapromotion.com

Just log on and scroll down to:

SMASHWORDS NEWS

Progress Record

Date & time started: _____

Date & time completed: _____

Book Promotion Opportunity #27

Kindle Publishing Made Easy

While Smashwords has formed an agreement with Google and Apple, they still have not been accepted by Amazon. Smashwords does convert your ebook into the Kindle format, but you ALSO have to submit your file to Amazon directly.

Have you tried to format your book for Kindle and been frustrated with the result? Maybe you've read the instructions on the Internet on how to publish a Kindle book or seen some videos and just "don't get it"? **It's NOT your fault that you "don't get it"!**

You are nowhere near alone! There are countless thousands just like you, who have struggled with "How do I publish a Kindle book?" or "Why doesn't it work for me?" For everyone who teaches the art of publishing Kindle books, for all the "getting results" people there are, I assure you there are many more who just can't seem to get the hang of it!

Is there a solution to the problem of "not getting it"?

After all, you've seen the video tutorials, you've read the testimonials, heard the audios. In fact, you probably can't escape from the numbers of people telling you how great their lives have become since they started selling Kindle books by the ton.

Introducing: "The Step-by-Step Guide to Turning Any Book or eBook Into a Kindle Edition and Publishing It with Amazon's Kindle Direct Publishing."

To get the ebook, go to:
http://amzn.to/n2oROJ

Progress Record

Date & time started: _____

Date & time completed: _____

Book Promotion Opportunity #28

Smashwords Style Guide

*T*he *Smashwords Style Guide* has helped thousands of authors produce and publish high-quality ebooks from a Microsoft Word .doc file.

This free guide offers simple step-by-step instructions to create and format an ebook. It's required reading for any author who wants to distribute their book via Smashwords to major ebook retailers such as the Apple iBookstore, Barnes & Noble, Sony, Kobo, and Diesel.

It's been recently updated with new troubleshooting information for building linked Tables of Contents and NCXes. What's an NCX, you ask? An NCX provides enhanced navigation for .ePub ebook customers. (See Step 20 in the style guide.)

The guide is available in English and several other languages. No charge. Download now in your choice of formats. http://www.smashwords.com/books/view/52

Progress Record
Date & time started: _____
Date & time completed: _____

Book Promotion
Opportunity #29

Foreign Rights

Foreign rights agents find the best international publishers, show your books, negotiate the contract, monitor the sales, and collect the royalties.

We have two outstanding rights agents with solid track records. Call and interview each one:

Godfrey Harris

Do you want to sell your books through foreign distributors, attract international library sales, market your foreign translation, or reprint rights? To learn what is involved in today's marketing climate, get in touch with Godfrey Harris, Executive Director Emeritus of International Publishers Alliance, a former U.S. diplomat, and a specialist on international book sales at:

hrmg@mac.com

+1-310-476-6374

Bob Erdmann

Foreign Rights veteran Bob Erdmann and his Columbine Communications has two foreign rights programs. They are:

- AWARD-WINNING BOOKS PROGRAM. This program features nonfiction titles that have won awards for their meaning and usefulness to readers. On behalf of our clients, we reach out to thousands of foreign publishers and agents. There is limited space for this promotion in order to provide prominent exposure of participating books.

- ANNUAL CATALOG PROGRAM. Our Annual Foreign Rights Catalog features nonfiction books in business, psychology, self-help, personal development, relationships, parenting, health, education, and other selected nonfiction titles. Our Annual Foreign Rights Catalog is the preeminent rights guide referred to by thousands of foreign publishers and agents each year seeking commendable books for foreign rights.

Contact Bob Erdmann at

bob@bob-erdmann.com

+1-209-586-1566

Progress Record

Date & time started: _____

Date & time completed: _____

Book Promotion Opportunity #30

Photo Sources

Whether you are publishing fiction or nonfiction, illustrations make the book more interesting. Fiction can benefit from maps and location photos. Nonfiction—well, a picture is worth a thousand words.

Some sources offer copyright-free illustrations at no charge. Others cost a modest amount. Illustrations may be used in books, news releases, brochures, PowerPoint shows, and so on.

Creative Commons search draws from photo, illustration, videos, and  music sites and filters out all but the files that may be used for commercial purposes.

http://search.creativecommons.org

Flickr offers more than 200 million photographs  from Creative Commons that can be used for book covers and book interiors.

Go to:

http://www.flickr.com/search/advanced

Scroll down and check three boxes:
- "Only search within Creative Commons-licensed content,"
- "Find content to use commercially,"
- "Find content to modify, adapt, or build upon."

Then search by keywords to find free images to use in your marketing.

ClipArt has 10 million photos, clip art, sounds, and so on.  Clipart.com, by Getty Images, is the largest collection of royalty-free images offered by subscription on the web. For one low price you can download all the clip art, photos, fonts, and sounds you need.

Subscriptions are for the month, quarter, half-year, and year.

http://ClipArt.com

Progress Record

Date & time started: _____

Date & time completed: _____

Book Promotion
Opportunity #31

Writing Headlines

Writing headlines that draw eyeballs, minds, and wallets is an art, but you can get a cheat sheet—free. This short course is  fascinating and can be applied to chapter titles, back cover sales copy, and even book titles.

Learn great headline writing from an expert.
http://www.cormacmoore.com/wp-content/
uploads/2013/12/Headline-Hacks-08-18-2012.pdf

Progress Record
Date & time started: _____
Date & time completed: _____

Book Promotion
Opportunity #32

Cross-Channel Success

A free report that is fascinating, fact-filled, and will be life-changing. Leverage the power of email plus social media. If you're not engaging your customers via social channels as well as through email, you're not reaching your audience where it lives, works, and plays.

Email + Twitter + Facebook:
22 Tips to Cross-Channel Success

http://www.slideshare.net/diegomaccia/
email-twitter-facebook-22-tips-to-crosschannel-success

Progress Record

Date & time started: _____

Date & time completed: _____

Book Promotion Opportunity #33

eBook Publishing

*T*he *Secrets to eBook Publishing Success,* by Mark Coker, reveals the best practices of the most commercially successful self-published ebook authors. This ebook is a must-read for every writer, author, publisher, and literary agent.

Discover more than 25 best practices you can implement today at no cost. These secrets will help you become a more professional, more successful writer and publisher.

Share the secrets! Price: Free

https://www.smashwords.com/books/view/145431

Progress Record

Date & time started: _____

Date & time completed: _____

Book Promotion
Opportunity #34

Ingram News & Updates

Get the latest information on what is happening in book wholesaling ebooks and Print-on-Demand (POD).

http://www.ingramcontent.com/
pressreleases/Pages/home.aspx

Progress Record
Date & time started: _____
Date & time completed: _____

Book Promotion Opportunity #35

Stewart News Release Tips— Discover Great Book Publicity

This free tutorial of 89 lessons shows you how to write and distribute news releases the new

way—not only for journalists, but for potential customers and anyone else who needs what you are promoting. It's the best tutorial you'll find anywhere.

Once a day, for 89 days in a row, Joan Stewart will email you a lesson on how to write or distribute a news release that anyone who is interested in your topic, including the media, will read. This is the real meat of the tutorial and the part most people struggle with—even professional PR people.

You'll learn not only the basics of good news release writing for online and offline publicity, but you'll also see examples of good and bad press releases.

http://www.89pressreleasetips.com/

Progress Record
Date & time started: _____
Date & time completed: _____

Book Promotion Opportunity #36

Book Nutter

Book Nutter tweets information about your book. All you need to do is fill in the short form at this website:

http://booknutter.heroku.com/books

Be sure the suggested tweet you give them is compelling.

Progress Record
Date & time started: _____
Date & time completed: _____

Book Promotion Opportunity #37

Sips Card

Exposure: Submit your story to coffee drinkers. Sips Cards bring independent fiction and local coffee shop/bar venues together. Customers can find Sips Cards at participating coffee shop-like venues. Each card contains a QR code, loaded with a short story from an independent writer meant to last as long as their drink. The cards are venue specific and include their business information as well as that issue's author, story title, and website.

http://sipscard.com

There is a 3,000-word limit to all submissions. When submitting, indicate your name and submission title in your email. Multiple submissions are accepted.

http://sipscard.com/submit

Progress Record
Date & time started: _____
Date & time completed: _____

Book Promotion
Opportunity #38

Amazon Author Central

Click on:

> https://authorcentral.amazon.com/gp/
> home?ie=UTF8&referrer=KDP

Amazon says: Welcome to Author Central. We encourage you to add or update information about yourself for your Author Central Profile. Here's some quick links to important places:

Update Your Author Page

Add multimedia, blog feeds, a Twitter feed, or events to an Author Central Profile.

- View and edit your list of your books.
- Add a book to your bibliography.

Learn More

Self-publish your work to the Kindle for free and make up to 70% in royalties.

- Join Search Inside the Book.
- Become an Amazon Associate.
- See more free marketing and promotion resources at CreateSpace.

Add Book Extras and Set Your Title Apart!

Did you know that by adding Shelfari Book Extras to your title you may sell more books? Character descriptions, important places, awards, and much more should be completed to help make your book stand out. In addition to appearing on Kindle detail pages, Kindle customers can access Book Extras directly from a growing set of Kindle devices and Kindle reading applications.

- To add Book Extras to your title, follow these steps:
- Go to www.shelfari.com (an Amazon.com subsidiary).
- Log in using your Amazon.com username and password.
- In the top search bar, enter in your title name or author name.
- Locate your title from the search results.

Add, update, or correct the community-contributed set of Book Extras for your title.

Most publishers find that more than 80% of their book sales are through Amazon. It makes sense to enhance your books' listings there.

Progress Record
Date & time started: _____
Date & time completed: _____

Book Promotion Opportunity #39

KDP Select—Freebie Days

In 2012, I put two new books into Amazon's Kindle Direct Publishing (KDP) Select program.

KDP Select is a program implemented by online seller Amazon.com that allows independent authors and publishers to enroll their ebooks into Amazon's Kindle lending program.

Amazon provides your book with worldwide **availability**. Your book is listed free. You must promote your book to free ebook download sites, your own ezine list, blog, and so on—basically alert your readers to the free book.

When you make any of your titles exclusive to the Kindle Store for at least 90 days, authors with U.S. rights are automatically included in the Kindle Owners' Lending Library (KOLL) and you will earn your share of a monthly fund when readers borrow your books from the library. The monthly fund was $500,000 or $600,000 each month for 2012. So far, authors have earned more than $2.00 for each "lend."

You may continue to distribute your book elsewhere in *physical* format, or in any format other than digital, during the KDP Select 90-day promotion period. See:
http://kdp.amazon.com/self-publishing/KDPSelect

Once you enroll a book in KDP-S, you will receive more information from Amazon in a letter like this:

Hello from Amazon KDP!

The book "Writing Your Book" you recently submitted to KDP and enrolled in KDP Select has been published to the Kindle Store and is already available for readers to purchase here:
http://www.amazon.com/dp/B007VP66Z0

KDP Select allows you to enjoy benefits, such as earning a share of a monthly fund when readers borrow your book from the Kindle Owners' Lending Library and a promotional opportunity to offer your book as free to readers for up to 5 days every 90 days to expand your reach.

For more details on KDP Select, check out this page:
http://www.amazon.com/dp/B007VP66Z0

You can check on the current month's KDP Select fund by visiting your Bookshelf.

Also, you can find your book's number of borrows in real time through your Month-to-Date Unit Sales report here: https://kdp.amazon.com/select

Now that your KDP Select-enrolled book is live, you can manage its free promotion days in your Bookshelf by clicking the "Manage Promotions" link from the "Actions" menu or from the "Edit book details" page.

Your book's initial enrollment in KDP Select lasts for 90 days. For your convenience, *your book's enrollment will be automatically renewed for another 90 days,* unless you cancel automatic renewal by un-checking "Automatically renew this book's enrollment in KDP Select for another 90 days" box under "Enrollment Details" of your book before your book's current enrollment term expires. Take a peek below at other great author resources to help you sell more books:

Create a Dedicated Author Page for Yourself

If you are this book's author, increase your sales potential on Amazon by creating an Author Central account and share your most up-to-date information via a dedicated author page. Publishers, be sure to work with your authors to set up their Author Central accounts as well. Click the links below to create author pages on different marketplaces. Amazon.fr:

http://authorcentral.amazon.fr/kdp/B007VP66Z0

Amazon.de

http://authorcentral.amazon.de/kdp/B007VP66Z0

Amazon.co.uk

http://authorcentral.amazon.co.uk/kdp/B007VP66Z0

Amazon.com

http://authorcentral.amazon.com/kdp/B007VP66Z0

Create a Print Book with CreateSpace (A Member of the Amazon Group of Companies)

Create print editions of your book using CreateSpace's full array of services to help you self-publish and make your book available for sale to millions of potential customers on Amazon.com and other channels by visiting here.

Join Our KDP Community

We host KDP Forums, which are a great place to learn from others and share your experiences about independent publishing. See below to check them out:

http://forums.kindledirectpublishing.com/ kdpforums/index.jspa

If you need to update the price of your book, see below: https://kdp.amazon.com/self-publishing/ help?topicId=A2MLJ06E7JKXLN

Or see below for its descriptive information, such as title, author, or description:

https://kdp.amazon.com/self-publishing/ help?topicId=A2MLJ06E7JKXLN

For additional ideas on how to merchandise your book, be sure to check out the page at this link: https://kdp.amazon.com/self-publishing/ help?topicId=A37SMD4NYVZDI7

Thanks again for choosing KDP to publish your work; we wish you the best of luck in promoting and selling it!

Regards, Kindle Direct Publishing

KDP Select will be more successful if your ebook has ten or more 4- or 5-star reviews posted at Amazon. So, the preferred procedure is to upload your ebook to Amazon and to solicit reviews.

Then sign up for KDP Select and schedule some of your freebie days. Many authors report that 2 days, Friday and Saturday, are best. But the best days may depend on the audience for the ebook.

Next, notify the many sites that will announce your ebook as being free on those two days. Most will not list your ebook unless it has several multi-star reviews at Amazon. See above.

For a list of those sites and other information on KDP Select, see Amazon at:
http://amzn.to/LTlveI

Or Smashwords at:

https://www.smashwords.com/books/view/166860

By the way, this book, *KDP Select*, is not yet enrolled in Amazon's program.

At any time during your 90-day period, you may go to your account and elect not to continue for another 90 days.

Then you may upload your book to Smashwords, Booklocker, among other ebook retailers.

Progress Record
Date & time started: _____
Date & time completed: _____

Book Promotion Opportunity #40

Survey Monkey

Surveying your book's audience provides valuable information to you and positions you as a leader in your book's industry.

If you have a newsletter/ezine, you may distribute the survey to your subscribers—readers who already know you—and you may report on the findings of the surveys.

If you subscribe to a news release distribution service such as Mitchell Davis' Expert Click, you may report some of your findings in a news release and send readers back to your website for more information.

Refer to your book. See:

http://ExpertClick.com

And you can select a survey Q/A and turn them into an article to send to your book's industry publications. Refer to your book. See:

http://www.SurveyMonkey.com

You may ask up to ten multiple-choice questions and receive the first 100 replies free. If you want to expand on the number of questions or replies, there is a charge.

Unless you have a list of more than 20,000, 100 replies might be enough. Test. If you max out at 100, it may be worth your while to pay for more. See the Survey Monkey website for details.

Results will start coming in immediately. Just click on the Analyze Results tab to see the responses.

Survey Monkey will send you lessons on how to draft your questions and other lists you might use.

Survey Monkey will teach you a lot about people in your industry and will position you as a knowledgeable expert with the numbers.

Below is a survey we sent to authors and publishers of books. You may want to adapt some of these questions to your industry.

Book Publishing Survey Questions
Para Publishing

Computer. Do you use?

Microsoft Windows PC

Apple Mac

Other

Which book publishing forums (listservs) do you subscribe to?

Check all that apply.

Self-Publishing

Pub-Forum

SmallPub-Civil

PUBLISH-L

Fiction_L

POD Publishers

eBook-community

Who is your major dealer/wholesale buyer?

Which buys most of your books?

Amazon.com

Barnes & Noble (Brick & Mortar)

BarnesAndNoble.com

Book distributor such as NBN, IPG, Perseus

Accounting program. Which do you use?

Quicken

QuickBooks

Jaya123 (Al Canton)
Cat's Pajamas
Peachtree
Other
None

Association membership. (check all that apply)
Independent Book Publishers Association (IBPA)
Small Publishers Association of North America (SPAN)
Small Publishers, Artists and Writers Network (SPAWN)
Association of American Publishers (AAP)
Other

Personal. Do you consider yourself
An introverted writer
An extroverted book publicist

Category/Genre. You write and/or publish mostly
Fiction
Poetry
Nonfiction

Do you edit/publish/own a (check all that apply)
Blog
Forum
Ezine
Website

Employees.
> None (just you)
> 1-5
> 6-10
> 11-20
> 21 or more

Who do you publish?
> Yourself
> Other authors
> Both Yourself and other authors

Progress Record

Date & time started: _____

Date & time completed: _____

Book Promotion Opportunity #41

Review eBooks with Coupon Codes

Giving Away Books

To get a book to move up the sales charts, it has to be read, liked, and recommended. This is word-of-mouth, and personal recommendations have always worked.

Giving away books primes the pump only if you give the books to people who can *multiply* your effort. Don't give books to non-influential people who want the book for their own use. They can buy it.

Smashwords.com

Smashwords has a Coupon Code system for giving away review copies. Go to your book's listing at Smashwords, look on the right side, and click on "Manage this book's coupon."

This page allows you to assign coupon codes to ebooks, which you can then share with prospective customers on your fan email lists, your blog, website, your social networks, or in your news releases and other promotions.

Customers enter the code prior to completing their checkout to receive a discount (in this case 100%—free).

You can change or delete the code at any time and you can set a duration date. You have complete control over the (secret) code.

The invitation for a free ebook and the code may be emailed to book bloggers and anyone else who might review the ebook or otherwise multiply your investment.

The advantage to this system is that the reviewers can download the edition of their choice: PDF, ePub, Kindle, RTF, TXT, LRF, Palm, or reading online.

Book Bloggers

Giving copies of your book to book bloggers (on your book's subject) does multiply your investment because they have many dedicated subscribers who are already drawn to your book's subject.

Make a Google search for "book bloggers" + (your book's subject). Try several *subjects*.

KDP Select

One way to give away books is through Amazon's KDP Select program. This program has jumpstarted notoriety for several books. The drawback discussed by many program participants is that Amazon requires a 90-day exclusive on the title.

http://amzn.to/LTlveI

https://www.smashwords.com/books/view/166860

Book Fairs & Conventions

If you want to give the book away to book fair visitors or to a convention audience, you could hand out printed cards with pictures of the book's cover and author on the front side. The back will have a description of the book, your contact information, and end with the URL for the page at Smashwords with your book's listing and the coupon code. Also mention the expiration code for the coupon code.

Giving away an ebook is far less expensive and much easier than hauling paper books to an event.

At book fairs, book professionals often refuse free paper books because they are heavy and too much to carry. Imagine your next book fair—handing out cards instead of books.

Giving away books is a good investment. Reviews sell books and potential dealers need samples. Your book is its own ambassador. Don't let copies sit in your garage. Send them out; put them to work.

Coupon Codes make the process easy.

Progress Record
Date & time started: _____
Date & time completed: _____

Book Promotion
Opportunity #42

Shipping Supplies

Get your free priority mail regional rate shipping kit. When you're shipping **shorter distances** in the U.S., Priority Mail Regional Rate Boxes are the right way to ship for value. They eliminate the

per-pound price bumps typically found in zone-based shipping.

With Box A, you pay one rate per zone up to 15 lbs; Box B, one rate per zone up to 20 lbs; and with the larger Box C, you pay one rate per zone up to 25 lbs. Not only do they help reduce shipping costs—they also reduce the time you spend weighing boxes.

Choose between top- or side-loading boxes (top-loading only available for Box C). This service is available for Priority Mail Commercial Base and Commercial Plus™ customers.

Complete the form to get a free Priority Mail Regional Rate Shipping Kit with all five box sizes and a helpful tip sheet. One kit per customer per address.

https://regionalrate.com/step-register.aspx
https://www.prioritymail.com/regional_rates.asp

Progress Record
Date & time started: _____
Date & time completed: _____

Book Promotion Opportunity #43

List Your Book for Free in the "Family Friendly Book Directory"

In honor of the 12th anniversary of *I Love To Write Day*, John Riddle will be publishing the "Family Friendly Book Directory" and sending it to the 28,000 schools all across the U.S. that celebrate ILTWD every November 15. He will ask the school librarian to share the directory with the students, teachers, administrators, and parents. He will also send the directory to his ILTWD e-newsletter subscribers, and it will be posted at the following website:

www.ilovetowriteday.org

If you have a "family friendly" book (basically any book that does not contain excessive sex or violence), it can be listed FOR FREE! A free listing includes: name of book, author, price, and web address.

Paid ads are also available; you can include your book cover and 5 lines of copy.

Contact johnriddle@sprintmail.com if you want your book included in the directory as a FREE listing or a PAID one.

Progress Record
Date & time started: _____
Date & time completed: _____

Book Promotion
Opportunity #44

Paul Krupin's
Book Publicity Calendar

Each year publicity genius Paul Krupin creates an annual publicity plan to help people look ahead and map out their ideas for acquiring publicity throughout the year.

This unique publicity planner provides a month-at-a-glance roadmap to holidays and identifies the publicity lead time for each holiday.

The special design makes it easy to develop a detailed personalized framework of key dates and events so that you map out your strategy and ideas to promote your book or your writing.

http://blog.directcontactpr.com/2013/12/
publicity-planner-for-2014

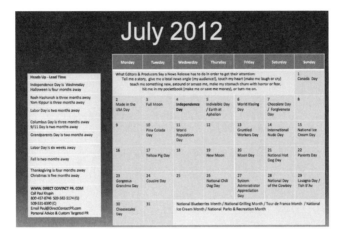

This calendar is for 2012. Contact Paul Krupin for a current one.

Paul Krupin, Personal Strategic Advice
    & Custom Targeted PR
800-457-8746 (TF)
509-582-5174 (O)
509-531-8390 (C)
Paul@DirectContactPR.com
www.directcontactpr.com
blog.directcontactpr.com

Progress Record

Date & time started: _____

Date & time completed: _____

Book Promotion Opportunity #45

Icons for Your Publications— Free Icon Finder

Thousands of public domain icons. Use in your ezine, books, PowerPoint, blog, and so on.

http://www.iconfinder.com

A fabulous resource.

Progress Record
Date & time started: _____
Date & time completed: _____

Book Promotion Opportunity #46

Bloggers Who Interview Authors

Bloggers are the new book reviewers. But you do not want to send books, ebooks, news releases, or make friends with just any blogger.

You should only be interested in book bloggers on your book's subject/genre/category. See this valuable list and add the bloggers who match your needs to your publicity list.

https://docs.google.com/spreadsheet/ccc?key=0AuE
e5VV8N4ZfdERiamRhVXhwY056THduOGV
OOHFyM1E#gid=0

Progress Record
Date & time started: _____
Date & time completed: _____

Book Promotion Opportunity #47

Convert ISBNs & Get Bar Codes

Converting ISBNs from 10-digit to 13-digit used to be a challenge. Bar codes used to be expensive. These resources will save you time and money.

Save this lesson for the next time you need ISBN conversion and/or barcodes.

Convert 10-Digit ISBNs to 13-Digit for Free

http://www.isbn.org/converterpub.asp

Get Barcodes for Free

Barcode Data:

(i.e. 780672318863)

Barcode Symbology: Code 128

Output Format: png

Generate Barcode

http://www.barcoding.com/upc/

http://www.tux.org/~milgram/bookland/

Progress Record

Date & time started: _____

Date & time completed: _____

Book Promotion
Opportunity #48

Information Kits

Offering free information kits on your book and its subject, and anything else you offer for sale, will save you a lot of time. And time is money.

Do you answer a lot of questions via email? Do potential clients give up trying to find what they want on your website? Are customers too short on time to read your blog?

Offering free InfoKits saves you time and conveys the info clients need—at the speed of light.

We send out close to 1,000 each week. And the process is automated. That helps clients and saves us time.

See (and download) our FREE InfoKits on book writing, production, and promotion. See how they work.

Free Information on Writing, Producing, and Promoting

We have three tip-filled, resource-laden Information Kits on writing, publishing and promoting books. Each kit is tailored to the experience/need level you specify. Fill in the form and you will receive a FREE kit immediately via email.

Request Form

[Items shown in red are required.]

Experience/need level:

◉ InfoKit #1, Writing: I am a writer working on a book.

◉ InfoKit #2, Publishing: I have finished my book and am ready to publish.

◉ InfoKit #3, Promoting: I have published and am working on promoting and distributing.

Email address must contain the "@" sign and no commas or spaces

Name

Zip Code if in the U.S. :

Or country if outside of the U.S. :

☐ **Please send me the free PublishingPoynters electronic newsletter**

[Submit Request Now!] [Reset Form Values]

Please tell your colleagues about these free Information Kits.

Privacy Notice: We will not distribute your email address to anyone. Period!

http://parapublishing.com/sites/para/
resources/infokit.cfm

Start off with a single page and grow it; add items to the page as the subjects come up. Setting up your InfoKit with an auto-responder is easy for a webmaster.

Your potential clients want your information and they like freebies. Do them a favor and do yourself a favor.

Progress Record
Date & time started: _____
Date & time completed: _____

Book Promotion
Opportunity #49

Outline on Book Promotion

John Riddle just updated the handout from his workshop, "50 Ways to Promote Your Book." You can have a free copy; just send an email to johne@sprintmail.com.

> "I am the author of 34 books and have worked as a ghostwriter on numerous projects. In 2002 I launched 'I Love To Write Day,' a grassroots campaign to have people of all ages practice writing every November 15. Last year more than 28,000 schools all across the U.S. held special ILTWD events and activities. Bookstores, libraries, writing groups, community centers, and even a few malls joined in the fun."

Write John and he will send you a free copy of *50 Ways to Promote Your Book*.

Progress Record

Date & time started: _____

Date & time completed: _____

Book Promotion Opportunity #50

Contests
(Written by Ellen Reid)

Want instant celebrity? Enter your book in a contest. Can you imagine how much buzz it generates for you to be able to say yours is an award-winning book?

There are all kinds of contests out there and many really want to support authors. It's no secret that my contests, that focus on overall excellence of a book, not just the writing, were created to assist authors in their success.

Here are some keys for submitting to contests:

- Pick the right category to enter—the one most closely aligned with your book's content. And consider entering in more than one category to increase your chances of walking away with an award. There's nothing wrong with being a double award-winner, either.

- Unless an award explicitly says they provide it, do not expect to get a critique of your book or an explanation for why your book was not chosen. I only mention this here so you go into this with awareness of what to expect.

- Whether it wins the gold, silver, or bronze medal, or your book is a winner or a finalist, it is still an award-winner. Any designation after "entrant" is a huge accomplishment and recognition. I suggest you let go of having to be the very best—only one book in a contest or category can have that distinction. And often, what puts a book there is beyond your control anyway. Recognize that receiving any level of award is a high honor and being *among* the best puts you in very good company.

- An award is an award. Don't be terribly concerned whether the award you enter is considered hugely prestigious or not. Yes, it's great to win the Nobel Prize for literature, or an Edgar for mysteries or a Hugo for Sci-Fi. But a sticker on your book from any legitimate award will go a long way—if you take advantage of it.

This last point brings me to another conversation. Just winning an award will not create buzz for your book. Winning gives you a powerful resource for promoting your book. Here are ways to leverage winning an award into book sales:

- Get stickers for your book cover and image files for your ebook. Stickers draw attention to your book and when browsers see yours has received an award, they will give it more consideration.

- Put the artwork for the award sticker or use a downloadable seal on your website. Make it prominent. Do the same on your social media pages as well as on your book's Amazon page.

- Tell the world. Send out a news release—be sure to use key search words in it. Because of the vast number of books reaching the marketplace each year, media producers often narrow their search to award-winners when looking for experts or guests.

- Announce your win in trade publications, like *Publisher's Weekly.*

- Alert your local media. Local papers are always looking for stuff to write about concerning local people. Send your news release to neighborhood news sheets, no matter how small. Google local publications—I guarantee you will find newspapers and magazines you never knew existed. And every mention of your book and you is a good thing.

- Send out emails—to everyone you know. This is not a time to be shy. Toot your horn. Sometimes learning your book won an award will push a friend who had been on the fence into a purchase.

• Add "Author of the award-winning *(Name of Book)*" or something like that to your email auto-signature. (If you don't have an email auto-signature, what are you waiting for? They're free and easy to set up!)

• Feature the award when you go to trade shows or events where you have a display.

• Have a poster or banner that highlights that yours is an award-winning book. Include the award sticker on the cover displayed in the poster.

• Put award stickers on flyers you send to bookstores.

• Mention the award when approaching book-reading clubs or groups you want to speak to.

Here are some awards you might consider:

• GLOBAL EBOOK AWARDS
www.globalebookawards.com

• NATIONAL INDIE EXCELLENCE AWARDS. Celebrating self-publishing excellence!
http://indieexcellence.com

- BEVERLY HILLS BOOK AWARDS (Books in print from all publishing houses). Celebrating excellence in print books from all publishers.
http://beverlyhillsbookawards.com

- USA REGIONAL EXCELLENCE BOOK AWARDS
http://usareba.com

- NAUTILUS BOOK AWARDS
www.nautilusbookawards.com

- BENJAMIN FRANKLIN BOOK AWARDS
ibpabenjaminfranklinawards.com

- NEXT GENERATION BOOK AWARDS
www.indiebookawards.com

- INDEPENDENT PUBLISHER BOOK AWARDS
www.independentpublisher.com/ipland/ipawards.php

and there are many more.

Progress Record
Date & time started: _____
Date & time completed: _____

Book Promotion
Opportunity #51

Program Wrap-Up

Congratulations! Not only did we provide you with more than 50 book promotion ideas, but implementing them taught you a lot about book promotion. You will be able to use these ideas again with future books.

What's new? Enhanced fiction ebooks. See my novel titled *Tailwinds*.

Thank you and best wishes for successful book promotion.

Dan Poynter

parapromotionbook.com